Designing Bird Feeders

Grades 3–5

Glenview, Illinois • Boston, Massachusetts • Chandler, Arizona • Upper Saddle River, New Jersey

ALWAYS LEARNING   PEARSON

Teacher Reviewers

Candida M. Braun
West Fargo Public Schools
West Fargo, North Dakota

Sherri M. Gibson
Union Elementary STEM and
Demonstration School
Gallatin, Tennessee

Susan Holt
Union Elementary STEM and
Demonstration School
Gallatin, Tennessee

L. Jean Jackson
Old Mill Middle South
Annapolis, Maryland

Paul Keidel
Bismarck Public Schools
Bismarck, North Dakota

Martin Laine
Ayer-Shirley Middle School
Ayer, Massachusetts

Angelia Joy Long
Charles Carroll Middle School
New Carrollton, Maryland

Linda McShane
La Grange Public Schools District 102
La Grange Park, Illinois

Diana Mitchell
Union Elementary STEM and
Demonstration School
Gallatin, Tennessee

Bradd Smithson
John Glenn Middle School
Bedford, Massachusetts

Mary Reid Thompson
Union Elementary STEM and
Demonstration School
Gallatin, Tennessee

Leslie Yates
Union Elementary STEM and
Demonstration School
Gallatin, Tennessee

Acknowledgments
Photographs
Every effort has been made to secure permission and provide appropriate credit for photographic material. The publisher deeply regrets any omission and pledges to correct errors called to its attention in subsequent editions.

Unless otherwise acknowledged, all photographs are the property of Pearson Education, Inc.

Photo locators denoted as follows: Top (T), Center (C), Bottom (B), Left (L), Right (R), Background (Bkgd)

Designing Bird Feeders
Cover: (R) ©Steffen Foerster Photography/Shutterstock, (L) ©Cosmin Manci/Shutterstock, (C) ©Radomir Jirsak/Shutterstock, (BC) ©Saulius L/Shutterstock; **ivB** (B) Eckehard Schulz/©Associated Press; **vB** (CR) Car Culture/Corbis; **viB** ©Mariusz Blach/Fotolia; **viiB** (BR) ©Fernando Blanco Calzada/Shutterstock; **viiiB** Courtesy, AeroVironment, Inc.; **ixB** ©Morris Mac Matzen/Reuters/Landov LLC; **xB** (BL) ©hotshotsworldwide/Fotolia, Thinkstock.

Building a Spirometer
Cover: (R) ©Henrik Lehnerer/Shutterstock, (CL) ©Johann Helgason/Shutterstock, (BL) ©Rob Byron/Shutterstock; **ivS** (B) Eckehard Schulz/©Associated Press; **vS** (CR) Car Culture/Corbis; **viS** ©Mariusz Blach/Fotolia; **viiS** (BR) ©Fernando Blanco Calzada/Shutterstock; **viiiS** NASA; **ixS** NASA; **xS** ©Monkey Business Images/Shutterstock.

Copyright © Pearson Education, Inc., or its affiliates. All Rights Reserved. Printed in the United States of America. This publication is protected by copyright, and permission should be obtained from the publisher prior to any prohibited reproduction, storage in a retrieval system, or transmission in any form or by any means, electronic, mechanical, photocopying, recording, or likewise. For information regarding permissions, write to Rights Management & Contracts, Pearson Education, Inc., One Lake Street, Upper Saddle River, New Jersey 07458.

PEARSON

ISBN-13: 978-0-13-319808-9
ISBN-10: 0-13-319808-1

Project STEM

Introduction to STEM
The Engineering Design Process . . . . ivB
What Is STEM? . . . . viB

Designing Bird Feeders
Introduction to Birds . . . . viiiB
Engineering Career *Robotic Birds* . . . . ixB
Technology *Spy Birds* . . . . xB
Quick Lab *Which Bird Beak Can Crush Seeds?* 1B
Vocabulary Practice 2B
Math Practice *Problem Solving Using Reasoning* 3B
Hands-on Inquiry *What Do Yeast Use for Energy?* 4B
STEM Project *Bird Food Is Served!* 5B
Technology Zone *Prosthetic Devices for Birds* 9B
Career Spotlight *Bioengineers and Animals* 11B
Enrichment *How Do Living Things Get Energy?* 13B
Assessment *Designing Bird Feeders* 14B
Performance Assessment *Designing Food for Birds* 16B
Standardized Test Prep 17B

Appendices
Safety Tips and Contract*

Making Measurements

Scientific Methods

Review the Safety Tips and Contract before beginning each topic.

The Engineering Design Process

Engineers are people who solve problems. They use the engineering design process described below to make new products. They may not follow these steps in the same order each time.

Identify a Need

When making a new product, engineers start by identifying a need or problem. Maybe a product is not working well. Maybe people need a new product. Engineers choose a problem or need to work on.

Research the Problem

Then, engineers gather information. They may find articles on the internet. They may find information in books and magazines. They may talk to other engineers. They might even conduct tests.

Design a Solution

Engineers use their research to find new solutions. Teams of engineers brainstorm ideas. During brainstorming, team members suggest design solutions. Often, one suggestion leads to other ideas.

As the team works, they take notes carefully. They write down all their ideas, sources, and material lists. They can use this information later if they need to. Or, others can use the notes to help them repeat the process.

Brainstorming usually results in many possible solutions. But engineers cannot build all these possible designs. They need to choose the best solution. To help them, they think about limits to their designs. Money and time are common limits.

Engineers also make trade-offs. In a trade-off, engineers trade one benefit of a design for another. For example, they might want to lower the cost of the product. To do this, they might use weaker materials. After making trade-offs and thinking about limits, engineers will choose the best solution.

Designing Bird Feeders

Build and Test a Prototype

Next, engineers build the solution they chose. This working model is called a prototype. Engineers test their prototype. They take measurements and collect data. Then they use the data to find out what works well. For example, they might try to find out if their solution is safe, sturdy, and easy to use.

Find Problems and Redesign

Engineers also test the model to find out what is not working well. They identify problems. They redesign the model to make it work better. Most designs need some changes before they are final.

Communicate the Solution

Engineers need to tell the people who build and use the product about the final design. They do this in different ways. They can make detailed drawings. They can write descriptions. They can organize their data in tables and graphs. Whatever they do, they must communicate their results in clear and precise ways.

What stage of the design process is this person completing?

What Is STEM?

At school, you probably have separate math classes, science classes, and English classes. But, can you use English in math class? Of course you can! You can use what you learn in one class to help you understand another. Applying what you learn is a big part of STEM: Science, Technology, Engineering and Math.

Science

Science is a way of learning about the world. Scientists observe nature.

They ask questions and conduct experiments to find out about nature.

They communicate their results to help us understand our world.

Technology

Technology is all around you.

It is not just computers and TVs.

Your pen, your pack, and even your shoes are examples of technology.

Technology is how people change the world to meet their needs.

STEM

Engineering

Engineering is using science to solve real-world problems.

Engineers find ways to meet our needs.

They apply scientific knowledge to build and improve technology.

You can use engineering to solve problems too.

Math

Math is a useful tool.

It can help you understand your data better. You can use charts and graphs to organize your data. You can use math to summarize your data.

People use math to solve problems in science, technology, and engineering.

Introduction

Birds

Hummingbirds got their name from the sound of their wings. They flap their wings so fast they make a small buzzing sound.

How many times can you flap your arms in one second? Can you flap them once? Twice? A hummingbird flaps its wings up to 200 times in a second. This helps hummingbirds fly with great speed—more than 30 mph. Hummingbirds are also the only birds that can fly backwards and upside down. Why? Hummingbird wings are built differently than the wings of other birds. The wings of most birds are mostly arm bones. Hummingbird wings have more hand bones. Their unique wings also allow hummingbirds to hover, or stay in one place in the air. Human beings can only do that if they are in a helicopter!

Take It Further

Go to the Journey North website for hummingbird migrations. Click on the pictures to read about the special traits of hummingbirds. Match the hummingbird traits with the human inventions that perform the same tasks.

Robotic Birds

Have you ever noticed that airplanes are shaped like birds? Airplane designers wanted a machine that flew as easily as birds do. Now those designers are learning to build machines that look even more like birds. Engineers study the bodies and movements of birds. They then experiment with materials and electronics to recreate what they learned. The result? Robotic birds. These robots look and fly like real birds. They take off and land by themselves. They flap their wings to move through the air. For now, engineers are still experimenting with mechanical birds. Still, robotic birds may be the wave of the future.

Engineers wanted this robotic bird to look like a sea gull. Did they succeed?

Take It Further

Engineers continue to create and test different types of bird robots. Use the Internet to research companies that are developing mechanical birds. Find out what skills and education are needed to work on these projects. Then use this information to create a help wanted poster.

STEM Connection: Technology

Spy Birds

A hummingbird buzzes around the room. It flies. It hovers. It lands on your head. That is when you realize you have been watching a robot. This hummingbird was designed to copy the appearance and movement of the real thing. It weighs two-thirds of an ounce. That's less than a AA battery. The bird carries a camera, a motor, batteries, and a communications system. Why? To spy! The hummingbird was created at the request of the United States military. The armed forces wanted a robot that could gather information without drawing attention. After all, a spy bird is far less noticeable than a spy plane.

Take It Further
The mechanical hummingbird was designed to be a mini spy plane. How else could it be used? Brainstorm ways such a robot could be helpful. Choose one use from your list. Make an advertisement for the bird that emphasizes your chosen use.

Hummingbirds are not found in some places on Earth. How could this fact limit the use of the mechanical hummingbird?

Name _____ Date _____

Quick Lab Which Bird Beak Can Crush Seeds?

☑ **1.** Make a model of a heron's beak. Glue 2 craft sticks to a clothespin. Use the other clothespin as a model of a cardinal's beak. Use pieces of a straw as models of seeds.

☑ **2.** Use the heron's beak. Pick up a seed. Does the beak crush the seed? Record.
_____

☑ **3.** Repeat with the cardinal's beak. Pick up a seed. Record.
_____

Materials
☐ 2 clothespins
☐ craft sticks
☐ glue
☐ 4 pieces of straw

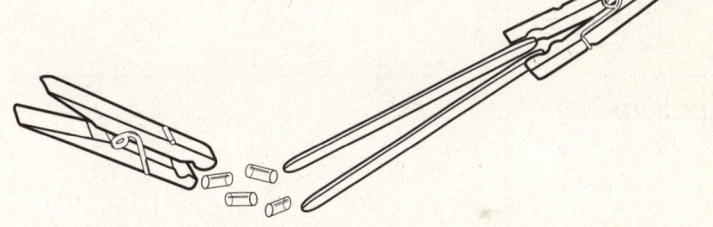

Explain Your Results

4. Draw a conclusion. Which bird beak crushes seeds?
_____

5. There are many seeds in a cardinal's environment. Infer how a cardinal's beak helps the cardinal survive.
_____
_____
_____

Designing Bird Feeders

Name _____ Date _____

Vocabulary Practice

Use your textbook or a dictionary to help write a definition for each term.

Word	What it means
adaptation	
habitat	
model	
pattern	
prosthetic device	
species	

Designing Bird Feeders

Name _____   Date _____

Math Practice Problem Solving Using Reasoning

You can use logical reasoning to find answers to problems. You may be able to determine more about a situation from the information given in the problem.

Izzy observes a bird feeder for 4 days. Twelve birds visit the bird feeder. Four birds were cardinals. He saw 2 more blue jays than robins. How many of each bird used the feeder?

What do I know?	What do I need to find out?	What can I determine from the information?
Twelve birds visited the bird feeder. 4 of the birds were cardinals. There were 2 more blue jays than robins.	How many blue jays visited the bird feeder? How many robins visited the bird feeder?	If 4 of the 12 birds were cardinals, the other 8 birds were a combination of blue jays and robins.

Take 8 two-color counters. Find combinations so that one color will have 2 more than the other. If you try 4 and 4, the difference is 0, so try 5 and 3. It works.

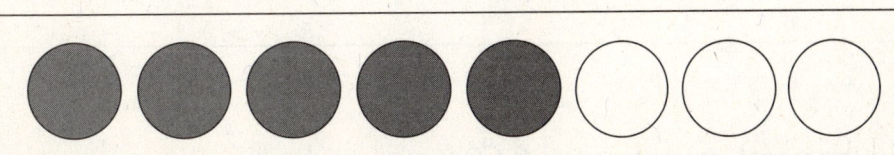

Solve.

1. Conor puts hay out for the animals on his ranch. He observes 13 animals in all eating the hay. 5 horses eat the hay. 6 more donkeys than pigs eat the hay. How many of each animal ate the hay?

   _____ horses _____ donkeys _____ pigs

2. Hunter plays 15 songs at his concert. He plays 3 songs on the violin. He plays 2 fewer songs on mandolin than on guitar. How many songs did Hunter play?

   _____ violin _____ mandolin _____ guitar

3B
Designing Bird Feeders
Copyright © Pearson Education, Inc., or its affiliates. All rights reserved.

Name _____ Date _____

Hands-on Inquiry What Do Yeast Use for Energy?

Yeast are tiny living things. They cannot make their own food.

☑ 1. Put ½ spoonful of yeast in a cup. Fill the cup half full with warm water. Stir. Observe for 10 minutes.

☑ 2. Add 1 spoonful of sugar to the cup. Stir. Observe for 10 more minutes.

Materials
☐ plastic cup
☐ yeast
☐ warm water
☐ 2 spoons
☐ sugar

Explain Your Results

3. Compare what you observed before and after adding sugar.

_____
_____
_____

4. What did the yeast use for energy? Cite your evidence.

_____
_____
_____

5. How did the yeast use the sugar to create energy?

_____
_____
_____

Designing Bird Feeders

Name _____ Date _____

STEM Project

Bird Food Is Served!

The food that birds eat depends on the type of bird and what is available. Birds may eat seeds, insects, or even rodents. Many people enjoy watching birds and hearing their cheerful songs. A well-built and well-placed bird feeder is an invitation that most birds cannot turn down. The area bird-watching club has asked you to design and build a bird feeder that a specific species of bird can enter.

Identify the Problem

☑ **1.** What problem will your bird feeder address? _____

_____

_____

Do Research Examine the chart below.

Species	Size of Base (cm)	Height (cm)	Entrance Above Base (cm)	Diameter of Entrance (cm)	Height Above Ground (m)
Bluebird	13 x 13	25	20	3.8	1.5–3.5
Chickadee	10 x 10	20–25	15–20	2.9	2.0–4.5
Nuthatch	10 x 10	20–25	15–20	3.2	4.0–6.0
House Wren	10 x 10	15–20	3–15	2.5–3.2	2.0–3.0
Tree Swallow	13 x 13	15	3–15	3.8	3.0–5.0
Purple Martin	15 x 15	15	2.5	6.4	5.0–6.0
Downy Woodpecker	10 x 10	23–30	15–20	3.2	2.0–6.0

☑ **2.** Why might different species of birds require different-sized feeders? _____

_____

Designing Bird Feeders

STEM Project

Name _____ Date _____

☑ **3.** Why does it matter how big the entrance is and how far it is above the base?

_____
_____

☑ **4.** Why does it matter how high the feeder is above the ground? _____

_____
_____

☑ **5.** Research the kinds of birds in your area and list three that are also listed in the chart.

1. _____
2. _____
3. _____

☑ **6.** Examine pictures of the birds you listed. Describe your observations.

1. _____
2. _____
3. _____

Go to the materials station(s). Look at each material. Think about how it may or may not be useful for building your feeder. Leave the materials where they are.

☑ **7.** What are your design constraints?

_____
_____

6B

Designing Bird Feeders
Copyright © Pearson Education, Inc., or its affiliates. All rights reserved.

Name _____ Date _____ **STEM** Project

Develop Possible Solutions

☑ **8.** Decide which type of bird you will try to attract to your feeder. Describe two different ways that you could use the materials provided to build a bird feeder for this type of bird.

_____
_____

Choose One Solution

☑ **9.** Decide which feeder you will make. Draw a diagram of your feeder. Label all the parts, including dimensions of holes you will make or lengths of perches.

☑ **10.** List the materials you will need. _____
_____
_____

☑ **11.** Tell what kinds of seed you will use to attract birds to your feeder. _____
_____

Design and Construct a Prototype

Gather your materials plus a metric ruler. Build your bird feeder.

☑ **12.** Record the design details of your prototype. _____
_____
_____

Designing Bird Feeders

STEM Project

Name _____ Date _____

Test the Prototype

Test your bird feeder. Find a place outside your classroom or home to place the feeder. Fill your feeder with the appropriate feed for the kind of bird you want to attract, supplied by your teacher. Observe your feeder for seven days. Record your observations in the chart.

Day	Observations
1	
2	
3	
4	
5	
6	
7	

Communicate Results

☑ **13.** Did your prototype work like you expected? Explain. _____
_____

☑ **14.** Compare your results with those of your classmates. How do your results compare?
_____

Evaluate and Redesign

☑ **15.** What were the flaws in your design? _____
_____

☑ **16.** What changes could you make to your design to make it better? _____
_____

Designing Bird Feeders

Name _____ Date _____

Technology Zone Prosthetic Devices for Birds

Being a bird isn't easy. Birds can be prey for other birds, animals, and humans. Birds, like all animals, can be injured. A bird will have trouble eating if it has an injured beak. A bird with an injured leg will find it hard to get around and avoid danger.

Bioengineers and veterinary surgeons often work together to make prosthetic devices for injured birds. A prosthetic device is any artificial device that replaces a body part. Before bioengineers can design a prosthetic beak or claw, for example, they need to understand how birds use their beaks and claws.

Birds need their beaks to eat, drink, hunt, and protect themselves. They also need beaks to preen, or clean their feathers. Bioengineers have created prosthetic beaks like the one on this eagle. The beaks are made of strong, light materials, like titanium. They need to be light so they don't hurt the bird's neck.

Bioengineers have also created prosthetic feet for birds like the one shown below. Prosthetic feet allow a bird to walk, to perch, and to avoid predators. An avian veterinarian fitted a badly injured cockatoo with prosthetic legs, saving the bird's life and allowing her to walk again.

Prosthetic devices for birds and animals can help protect endangered species. The things bioengineers learn with these experiments also help them make better prosthetic devices for people.

Name _____   Date _____

Check Your Understanding

1. How is making a prosthetic leg for a bird the same as making one for a person? How is it different?

   _____

   _____

   _____

2. How can work on prosthetic devices for animals help people?

   _____

   _____

3. Imagine you are making a prosthetic leg for a bird. Draw the bird and the prosthetic leg. What materials would you use to build the leg? Choose at least 3 different materials. Draw arrows to show which part of the leg you would use them for. Write a sentence about why you chose each one.

10B
Designing Bird Feeders
Copyright © Pearson Education, Inc., or its affiliates. All rights reserved.

Name _____   Date _____

Career Spotlight Bioengineers and Animals

How can studying geckos lead to better surgery on humans?

Biology is the study of living things. Bioengineers study both biology and engineering. They use engineering to work with living things.

Some bioengineers use technology to help animals. For example, they make prosthetic devices for wounded animals.

Other bioengineers learn from nature to create technology for humans. Some people study birds and insects to understand how they fly. This helps them design better airplanes. For example, owls fly very quietly. Scientists have studied owls to discover how to make quieter airplanes. Hummingbirds fly with quick and exact movements. They can hover in the air in one spot. Engineers have studied them to design mechanical devices that can be used for spying.

Other animals have different adaptations that we can learn from. The gecko, a type of lizard, can walk up and down walls and windows. Its feet can stick to just about any surface. Then the gecko can easily pull its feet back up again when it wants to. Engineers have studied geckos' feet like the one shown below to learn how to make better glue and tape. One invention is a super-strong waterproof bandage that might be used to seal organs after surgery. The secret to the bandage was found to be in the tiny hills and valleys found on the gecko's feet.

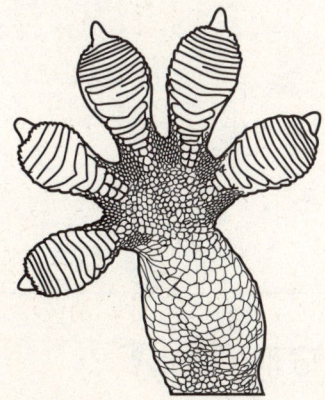

By studying both biology and engineering, bioengineers are able to help both animals and people.

Designing Bird Feeders

Name _____ Date _____

Check Your Understanding

1. What are some other ways bioengineers can help animals?

_____

_____

2. Name two things that animals can do but people can't. Think of some technologies that could be developed from studying these animals. Draw one animal adaptation and the technology.

```
┌─────────────────────────────────────────────┐
│                                             │
│                                             │
│                                             │
│                                             │
│                                             │
│                                             │
│                                             │
│                                             │
│                                             │
│                                             │
└─────────────────────────────────────────────┘
```

3. How do you think owls are able to fly silently?

_____

_____

12B

Designing Bird Feeders
Copyright © Pearson Education, Inc., or its affiliates. All rights reserved.

Name _____ Date _____

Enrichment How Do Living Things Get Energy?

Sunlight provides the energy for plants. Plants make their own food with energy from the sun. Plants are *producers*. Animals get their energy from eating plants or from eating other animals. Animals are *consumers*.

Draw arrows to show which way the energy flows in this food chain.

1. Where does the energy begin in this food chain? _____

2. Who are the producers in this food chain? _____

3. Who are the consumers in this food chain? _____

4. Do you think the raccoon is the end of this food chain? Explain.
_____

5. Think of other animals and plants that form a food chain. Draw your food chain. Label the plants and animals. Write *producer* or *consumer* below each one.

13B
Designing Bird Feeders

Name _____ Date _____

Assessment Designing Bird Feeders

Complete each sentence with the correct word.

1. All _____ are consumers. (plants, animals)

2. Energy can flow through an ecosystem from a producer to a _____. (producer, consumer)

3. A bird's bill is a(n) _____ that helps it meet its need for food. (hibernation, adaptation)

4. Pelicans eat fish. A pelican's beak has a pouch that hangs from it. How does this adaptation help it survive?

   _____

   _____

   _____

5. Draw a food chain that shows grass, a hawk, the sun, a mouse, and a snake. Label each organism as a producer or consumer.

14B
Designing Bird Feeders
Copyright © Pearson Education, Inc., or its affiliates. All rights reserved.

Name _____ Date _____

6. A bird has a long narrow beak. It eats bugs that live under the bark of trees. What kind of habitat does it probably live in?

    a. at the beach

    b. in a grassy meadow

    c. in the woods

    d. in a place with a lot of flowers that have seeds

How do you design bird feeders for different kinds of birds?

7. Suppose you want to attract finches. Finches are a small bird that eat very small seeds such as thistles. Design a feeder for finches. Draw it here.

What else do you need to know before you set up your feeder?

_____

_____

15B
Designing Bird Feeders

Name _____ Date _____

Performance Assessment
Designing Food for Birds

Different birds can eat different kinds of food. Small birds such as finches and sparrows prefer bread crumbs, smaller seeds like thistles, and plant shoots. Larger birds such as blue jays and cardinals prefer larger seeds like sunflower seeds for food. Birds such as turkeys and ducks love to eat whole corn seed.

You have to design a mixture of seeds to use with your bird feeder. Consider what kind of bird(s) you want to attract. Research the types of seed it prefers to eat.

Design It

1. What types of birds do you want to attract?
   _____
   _____

2. What kind of seed mixture will you design? Write your seed mixture as a recipe.
   _____
   _____
   _____
   _____

3. After testing your seed mixture, what will you redesign to make it work better?
   _____
   _____
   _____
   _____

Name _____ Date _____

Standardized Test Prep

Circle the letter of the best answer.

1. What is the first step of the design process?

   A Do research.

   B Identify the problem.

   C Choose one solution.

   D Construct a prototype.

2. The long beak of a heron is one example of an adaptation. This adaptation helps

   A the heron be a better producer.

   B the heron survive in its environment.

   C the heron be a model for other birds.

   D the heron survive without a prosthetic device.

3. How is the design of a bird feeder important for the species of birds that will use the bird feeder?

   A The design of the bird feeder is not important because all bird species can use the same design.

   B The bird feeder must contain a prosthetic device for some species.

   C The bird feeder must be specially designed for the type of species that will use the feeder.

   D The design of the bird feeder must have adaptations for all species.

Lab Safety

Always follow these rules to stay safe in the science lab.

- Read the activity carefully before you start.
- Listen to the teacher's instructions. Ask questions about things you do not understand.
- Keep you work area neat and clean. Clean up spills right away.
- Never taste or smell any substance unless directed to do so by your teacher.
- Handle sharp items and other equipment carefully.
- Use chemicals carefully. Dispose of chemicals properly.
- Help keep plants and animals that you use safe.
- Tell your teacher if there is an accident or if you see anything that looks unsafe.
- Wash your hands when you are finished.
- Wear safety goggles and gloves when necessary.
- Tie back long hair.

Look for this stop sign in your book. It warns you that you need to be careful. Follow the directions after the sign to stay safe in the lab.

Laboratory Safety Contract

I, _____,
          (print full name)

have read the Laboratory Safety Rules. I understand their contents completely. I agree to follow all safety rules and guidelines for each of the following categories:

(please check)

- ▢ Wear safety equipment when necessary.
- ▢ Listen to the teacher.
- ▢ Report accidents immediately.
- ▢ Handle tools carefully.
- ▢ Keep my workplace clean.
- ▢ Clean up spills.
- ▢ Wash my hands after an activity.
- ▢ Use chemicals carefully.
- ▢ Keep plants and animals safe.

_____
          (signature)

Date _____

Making Measurements

Scientists use measurements to record precise observations. They also use measurements to communicate their findings.

Measuring in SI

Scientists use the **International System of Units (SI)** as their standard system of measurement. SI units are easy to use. Each unit is ten times greater than the next smallest unit. The table lists some SI prefixes. These prefixes name the most common SI units.

Common SI Prefixes

Prefix	Symbol	Meaning
kilo-	k	1,000
hecto-	h	100
deca-	da	10
deci-	d	0.1 (one tenth)
centi-	c	0.01 (one hundredth)
milli-	m	0.001 (one thousandth)

Mass

Mass is measured in **grams (g)**. Mass is the amount of matter in an object. One gram is about the mass of a paper clip. Larger masses are measured in kilograms (kg). Scientists use a balance to find the mass of an object.

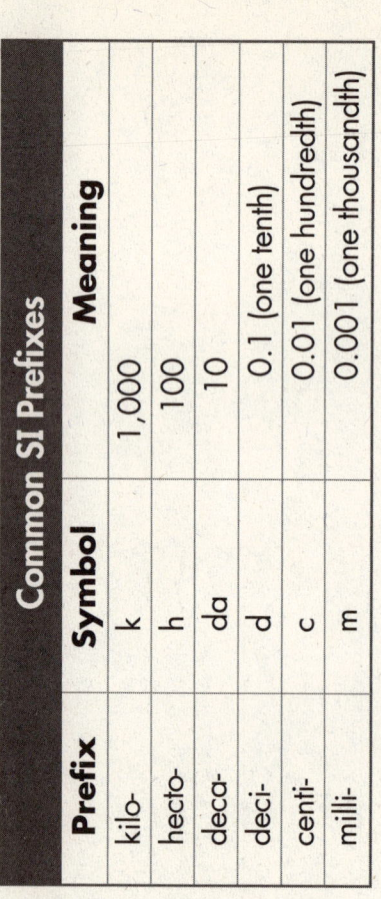

The mass of the potato is 0.25 kg or 250 g.

Common Conversion

1 kg = 1,000 g

Temperature

Scientists use the **Celsius scale** to measure temperature. Temperature is recorded in degrees Celsius (°C). Water freezes at 0°C and boils at 100°C. Scientists measure temperature using a thermometer.

The temperature of the water is 35°C.

Length

Length is measured in **meters (m)**. Length is the distance between two points. The distance from the floor to a doorknob is about one meter. Long distances are measured in kilometers (km). Short distances are measured in centimeters (cm) or millimeters (mm). Scientists use metric rulers and meter sticks to measure length.

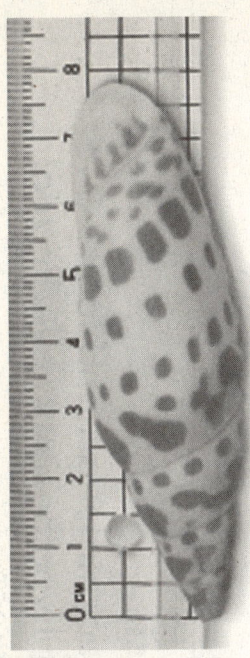

This shell is 7.8 cm or 78 mm.

Common Conversions

1 km	=	1,000 m
1 m	=	100 cm
1 m	=	1,000 mm
1 cm	=	10 mm

Liquid Volume

Liquid volume is measured in **liters (L)**. Liquid volume is the amount of space a liquid takes up. One liter is about the volume of a medium-size milk container. Smaller volumes are measured in milliliters (mL). Scientists use graduated cylinders to measure liquid volume.

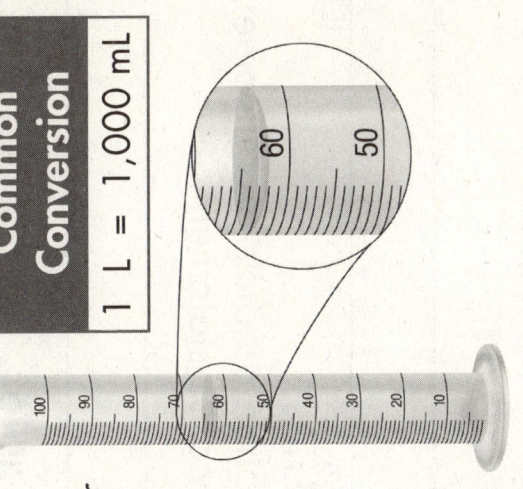

The volume of water in the graduated cylinder is 62 mL.

Common Conversion

| 1 L | = | 1,000 mL |

Time

Scientists measure time in **seconds (s)**. Time is how long something takes. There are 60 seconds in one minute. Longer times are measured in hours or days. Scientists use stopwatches and timers to measure time.

Common Conversions

| 1 hour | = | 60 minutes |
| 1 minute | = | 60 seconds |

Scientific Methods

Scientific methods are organized ways to answer questions and solve problems. Scientific methods help scientists draw conclusions. Scientists do not always use the same methods.

Ask a question.

Ask a question that you want answered. You might have a question about something you observe.

State your hypothesis.

A hypothesis is a possible answer to your question. It often predicts an outcome of an experiment. Write it as an *If...then...because* statement.

Identify and Control Variables.

Variables are things that can change. For a fair test, choose just one variable to change. Keep the other variables the same.

Test your hypothesis.

Make a plan to test your hypothesis. Collect materials and tools. Then follow your plan. Each time you test your hypothesis is called a trial. Repeat each trial three times.

 **Collect and record your data.** Keep good records of what you do and find out. Use tables and pictures to help.

 **Interpret your data.** Organize your notes and records to make them clear. Make diagrams, charts, or graphs to help.

 **State your conclusion.** Your conclusion is a decision you make based on your data. Communicate what you found out. Tell whether your data supported your hypothesis.

 **Try it again.** Do the experiment a few more times. The results of one experiment might not be right. Be sure to do everything exactly the same each time.

Name _____ Date _____

Name _____ Date _____

STEM GLOSSARY

Name _____ Date _____

STEM GLOSSARY

Name _____ Date _____

Standardized Test Prep

Circle the letter of the best answer.

1. What is a spirometer designed to measure?

    A The amount of air you exhale.

    B The amount of oxygen you inhale.

    C The amount of oxygen you exhale.

    D The amount of carbon dioxide you inhale.

2. The function of the respiratory system is to

    A digest the food you eat.

    B supply your blood with oxygen.

    C protect your body from foreign substances.

    D transport oxygen throughout your body.

3. Which of the following is a problem that biomedical engineers might be asked to solve?

    A A biomedical engineer might be asked to design a car that gets better gas mileage.

    B A biomedical engineer might be asked to design a light bulb that gives off less heat.

    C A biomedical engineer might be asked to design a fabric that resists stains.

    D A biomedical engineer might be asked to design artificial skin that reduces scar tissue.

Name _____ Date _____

Performance Assessment
A Spirometer for Everyone

A pulmonologist at a medical clinic has seen your spirometer and wants one that can test the breathing capacity of many patients.

You have to redesign your spirometer so many different people can use it. Hygiene is important because the doctors do not want patients getting each other sick.

Design It

1. **Redesign** List any design changes you will need to make to your current model so it can be used by many people.

   _____

   _____

2. What materials would you use? Explain how you chose these.

   _____

   _____

3. Draw your new spirometer design. Your drawing should be clear enough that another person could build a prototype of it. Label all the parts.

Building a Spirometer

Name _____   Date _____

4. Suppose you are planning the amount of air needed for a space trip. You need to know your breathing rate while you are sitting still and while exercising. Why is it important to know your breathing rate while exercising? (Circle the correct answer.)

   a. Your body uses oxygen only when you exercise.

   b. When you exercise you use more oxygen, and if you do not plan for this you may run out.

   c. When you exercise you use less oxygen, and if you do not plan for this you may take too much.

   d. There is already oxygen that you can breathe in space; you need more only if you exercise.

5. To carry out respiration, what do animals need from the air? (Circle the correct answer.)

   a. water vapor

   b. oxygen

   c. hydrogen

   d. carbon dioxide

6. When you exhale, you breathe out _____, which is a gas that plants need to live.

7. Plants are important to people on Earth. Plants are so important that astronauts even take them into space. Why do you think plants are so important to people on Earth and in space?

   _____
   _____
   _____

Building a Spirometer

Name _____ Date _____

Assessment Building a Spirometer

1. Use mental math to answer the questions. Justin records a breathing rate of 32 breaths a minute. How many breaths will he take in

   1 hour? _____

   5 hours? _____

   50 hours? _____

2. Why does a spirometer measure the amount of air you exhale, instead of the amount of air you inhale? (Circle the correct answer.)

   a. It is difficult to measure the amount of air you inhale.

   b. The volume of air you inhale is the same as the volume of air you exhale.

   c. Both a and b are true.

   d. None of the above are true.

3. Which of these might a biomedical engineer design? (Circle the correct answer.)

   a. a space hospital for astronauts while they are in space

   b. an artificial kidney for a sick person

   c. a new type of liquid air tank for space travel

   d. a thermometer for animals

Building a Spirometer

Name _____ Date _____

Enrichment Your Respiratory System

Your respiratory system is at work when you smell, talk, walk, and breathe. The job of your respiratory system is to carry gases between the outside air and your blood. The respiratory system allows oxygen to enter the blood. It also allows carbon dioxide to leave the blood.

Use the words in **dark type** to fill in the blanks next to each number. Decide where each word belongs. They will not be in order.

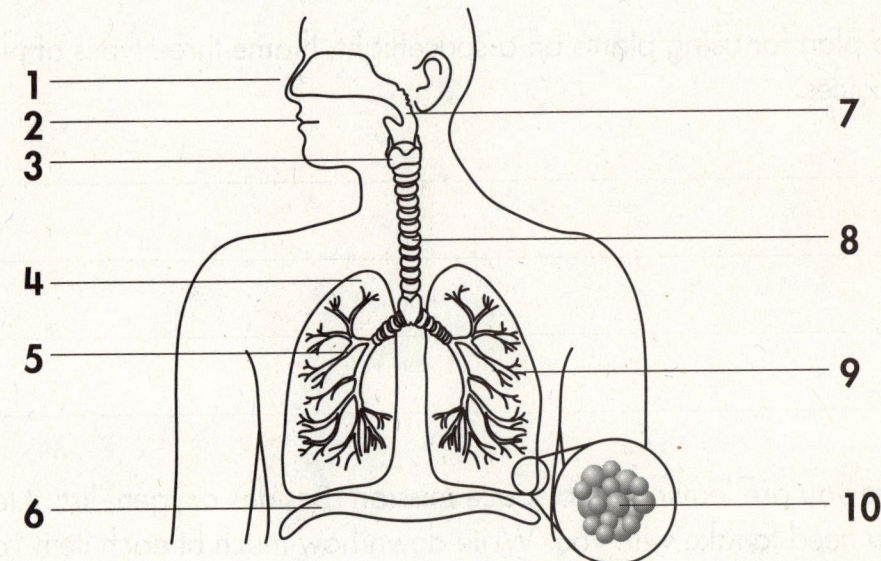

You breathe through your **nose** and **mouth**. You feel the air going down the back of your throat, in an area called the **pharynx**. However, breathing does not start with your nose or throat. It starts with a muscle below your lungs, called the **diaphragm**. When the diaphragm contracts, it pulls air into your **lungs**. When the diaphragm relaxes, the air flows back out.

After air enters your body, it continues down your chest in a stiff tube called the **trachea**, or windpipe. When the air enters the lungs, it spreads out through branching tubes called **bronchi**. These branch out into smaller tubes called **bronchioles**. Finally, the air enters tiny **air sacs** where it can mix with the blood.

At the top end of the trachea, there is another organ called the **larynx**. The larynx is also sometimes called the vocal folds or the vocal cords. By controlling the air that flows through your larynx, you can talk or sing.

Building a Spirometer
Copyright © Pearson Education, Inc., or its affiliates. All rights reserved.

Name _____ Date _____

Check Your Understanding

1. Suppose you take off in a rocket. The rocket's cabin is full of air. Why is this air not enough for a space trip? Give at least two reasons.

   _____
   _____
   _____

2. Make a plan for using plants on a spaceflight. Name three types of plants. Explain your choices.

   _____
   _____
   _____
   _____
   _____

3. Suppose you are leaving on a space mission. Besides oxygen, list at least 10 things that you need to take with you. Write down how much of each item you will need for a one-week trip.

   _____
   _____
   _____
   _____
   _____
   _____
   _____

Building a Spirometer

Name _____ Date _____

Technology Zone Getting Oxygen in Space

In outer space, there is no breathable oxygen. To travel into space, you need to take oxygen with you.

Our bodies need air that is about 20% oxygen and 80% nitrogen. This is the mixture that astronauts use, and it is close to what we breathe here on Earth.

Air is a gas and takes up a lot of space. You can't take entire roomfuls of air with you on a rocket or shuttle. This gas needs to be compressed so it takes up less space. Luckily, when you cool oxygen and nitrogen, you can turn them into a liquid. The liquid takes up only about 1/1,000 as much space as the gas! To keep the gas liquid, it has to be kept under pressure in a sturdy tank. The picture shows an oxygen tank used in a Saturn V rocket. To use the gas, you open a valve in the tank and allow some of the liquid to escape. As soon as it escapes the high pressure of the tank, it vaporizes, or turns back into a gas.

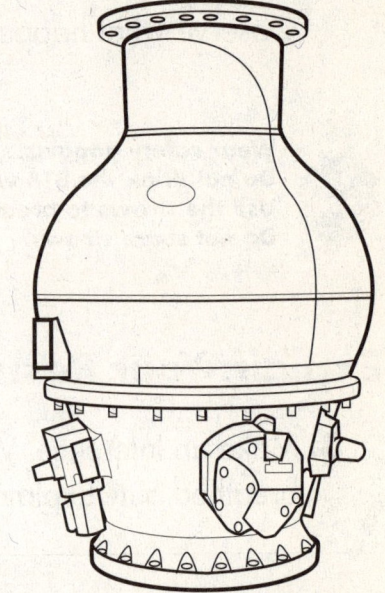

Besides taking enough oxygen with them, astronauts must also worry about the buildup of carbon dioxide. People exhale carbon dioxide. Too much carbon dioxide in the air can suffocate us. Fresh air has less than 0.05% carbon dioxide. If there is more than 2% carbon dioxide in the air we breathe, we might experience drowsiness, high blood pressure, and other problems.

In a closed space such as a rocket, the amount of carbon dioxide needs to be kept under 2%. One way to do this is by using chemical processes that remove carbon dioxide from the air. Plants can also help keep carbon dioxide levels safe on a spaceflight. Plants use carbon dioxide and release oxygen. During a long stay in space, plants can also provide fresh food for the astronauts.

Name _____ Date _____

Hands-on Inquiry What Do You Breathe Out?

Water with BTB will change from blue to pale yellow if carbon dioxide is added.

☑ **1.** Fill a cup $\frac{1}{3}$ full of water with BTB. Cover it with plastic. Push a straw through the plastic.

☑ **2.** Gently breathe OUT through the straw into the water. Observe what happens to the liquid.

Materials
☐ safety googles
☐ plastic cup
☐ water with BTB
☐ plastic wrap
☐ straw

**Wear safety goggles.
Do not drink the BTB water.
Use the straws to breathe OUT only.
Do not share straws.**

Explain Your Results

3. Make an Inference. Was there carbon dioxide in the air you breathed out? Explain using your observations.

_____
_____
_____

4. What conclusion can you draw about the body and carbon dioxide?

_____
_____
_____
_____
_____

Building a Spirometer

Name _____ Date _____

Check Your Understanding

1. How are biomedical engineers the same as other engineers, such as structural engineers who design bridges? How are they different?

_____

_____

_____

2. Think of two problems that biomedical engineers might be asked to solve. Then tell how they would solve the problems.

_____

_____

_____

3. Imagine you are designing a machine to replace an arm that was severely injured. What are some challenges that would make your work difficult?

_____

_____

_____

In the space below, draw your machine that would help a person with an injured arm.

Building a Spirometer

Copyright © Pearson Education, Inc., or its affiliates. All rights reserved.

Name _____ Date _____

Career Spotlight Biomedical Engineer

Have you ever heard anyone compare the human body to a machine? Like a machine, our body is made up of systems, such as the respiratory system. The systems work together to keep our body running. Like machines, though, our body can break down. This is where biomedical engineers come in.

Biomedical engineers design and develop products that help the human body function. For example, they might make devices that can help human organs work, or even replace them. They design pacemakers, which keep the heart beating at the right speed. They design insulin pumps, which help people with diabetes. They have designed hearing aids, replacement knees, and even artificial lungs.

Biomedical engineers are inventing new kinds of artificial lungs like the one in the picture below. These cannot completely replace human lungs, but they can help for a short period of time. Like human lungs, they take carbon dioxide out of blood and replace it with oxygen. Artificial lungs can be used for a few weeks while a patient's real lungs heal, or until a lung transplant can be made.

To design artificial lungs, biomedical engineers need to understand the respiratory system. They need to understand how fluids and gases flow. They also need to understand how machines work and how they can be safely connected to the body. Biomedical engineers need to work closely with doctors to make sure the machines are helping patients and not hurting them.

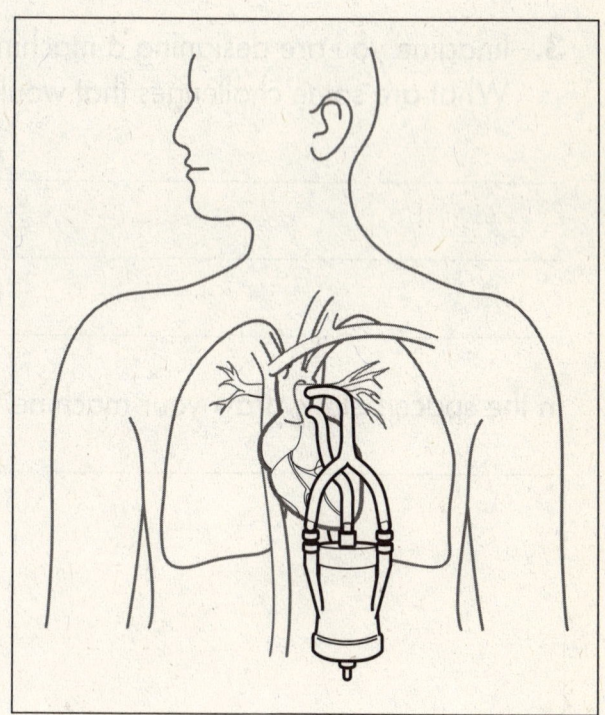

You may think that becoming a biomedical engineer sounds difficult, but it is a rewarding career. You need to understand both engineering and the human body very well. But the work you do helps people live better and longer lives.

Building a Spirometer

STEM Project

Name _____ Date _____

☑ **11.** Using the conversion of 1 liter = 1000 mL, convert your average tidal volume into liters. Show your work:

Tidal volume in liters = _____

☑ **12.** Use this average tidal volume in liters to calculate the total volume of air you would need for your two-day trip into space. Show your work:

Volume of air needed for two days in space (liters) = _____

Communicate Results

☑ **13.** Did your spirometer enable you to measure the volume of air you breathe in one breath? Explain. _____

_____

☑ **14.** Rate how well your spirometer worked using the scale below. Then explain why you gave the spirometer that rating.

    0 — did not work

    1 — worked but not very well

    2 — worked well

My spirometer prototype rating: _____

Explanation: _____

Evaluate and Redesign

☑ **15.** Explain how you would change your design to make it better. _____

_____

_____

Building a Spirometer

Name _____ Date _____   **STEM** Project

Choose One Solution

☑ **9.** Compare sketches with your group. Talk about your ideas and decide what kind of spirometer to build together. Describe your design here. Include an explanation of how the device will contain your exhaled breath and whether it will measure the volume of your breath.

_____
_____
_____

☑ **10.** List the materials that you will need.

_____
_____

Design and Construct a Prototype

Gather your materials. Build your spirometer.

Test the Prototype

Your first spirometer design is called your *prototype*. To test your prototype, inhale normally. Then exhale normally into the tubing connected to your spirometer. Be sure not to exhale forcefully. This is called your "tidal volume."

Do three trials and record your measurements in milliliters (mL). Calculate the average of your three trials in mL.

	Tidal Volume (mL)
Trial 1	
Trial 2	
Trial 3	
Average of three trials	

Building a Spirometer

Name _____ Date _____

Notes Grid

Building a Spirometer

Name _____ Date _____ **STEM** Project

☑ **5.** Which breathing rate should you use to calculate how much air you will need in space? Why? _____

_____

☑ **6.** Using the breathing rate you have chosen, calculate approximately how many breaths you take in an hour, in a day, and in two days. Show your work.

> 1 hr = 60 minutes
> 1 day = 24 hours

Breaths in one hour: _____

Breaths in one day: _____

Breaths in two days: _____

To determine the amount of air you will need, you can multiply the rate of your breathing by the volume of one breath. First you must capture the air you exhale in one breath and measure its volume. You will build a spirometer that captures this air and measures its volume.

Go to the materials station(s). Pick up each material, one at a time. Think about how it may or may not be useful in your design. Leave the materials where they are.

☑ **7.** What are your design constraints? _____

_____

Develop Possible Solutions

☑ **8.** Think of a way you could use the materials provided to build a spirometer to contain the air that you exhale and measure its volume. Draw a sketch showing your idea.

55
Building a Spirometer
Copyright © Pearson Education, Inc., or its affiliates. All rights reserved.

STEM Project

Name _____ Date _____

Breath of Life

With the right equipment, people can travel deep under the ocean's surface or high above Earth's atmosphere into space. Neither of these places has the air that people need to breathe. To make such a trip, people must take air with them. You can calculate how much air you need for a trip into space by finding how much air you inhale and exhale over a given period of time. You can do this using a spirometer. A spirometer captures the air that a person exhales in one breath and measures its volume.

Pretend you are an astronaut. You will design a spirometer to measure the volume of air you breathe. Then you will calculate how much air you would need to transport with you on a two-day journey into space.

Identify the Problem

☑ **1.** What is your task? _____
_____

Do Research

☑ **2.** While you are sitting still and breathing normally, count how many times you breathe in and out. Use a clock with a second hand or a digital seconds display to time yourself for one minute.

How many breaths did you take in one minute while at rest? _____

☑ **3.** Now do jumping jacks for one minute. Again count the number of breaths you take per minute.

How many breaths did you take in one minute while active? _____

☑ **4.** Compare the two breathing rates you found in questions 2 and 3. How do they differ? _____
_____

Building a Spirometer

Copyright © Pearson Education, Inc., or its affiliates. All rights reserved.

Name _____ Date _____

Math Practice Mental Math: Multiplying

Work with a partner. Discuss each question first. Then think about these equalities as you answer each question.

> 1 minute = 60 seconds
> 1 hour = 60 minutes
> 1 day = 24 hours

1. Rachel records her pulse for 30 seconds. She records 30 beats in 30 seconds. How many times will her heart beat in 1 minute? _____

2. How many times will her heart beat in 1 hour? _____

3. How many times will her heart beat in 1 day? _____

Use the results from your lab activity to answer questions 4–7.

4. How many times did your heart beat in 30 seconds? _____

5. How many times will your heart beat in 1 minute? _____

6. How many times will your heart beat in 1 hour? _____

7. Compare your results with your partner. Whose heart beats faster? _____

3S

Building a Spirometer

Name _____ Date _____

Vocabulary Practice

Draw a picture or write a sentence to go with each word. Use your science book or a dictionary to help.

Word	What it means
respiratory system	
pulse	
lungs	
volume	
spirometer	
measure	

Building a Spirometer

Name _____ Date _____

Quick Lab Observing Your Pulse

☑ **1.** Make a ball of clay. Push one end of a straw into the ball. Flatten the bottom of the clay.

Materials
☐ straw
☐ clay

☑ **2.** Rest your hand on a table with the palm up.

☑ **3.** Set the clay on your wrist near your thumb. Move the clay around until you observe the straw move.

☑ **4.** Describe the movements of the straw.

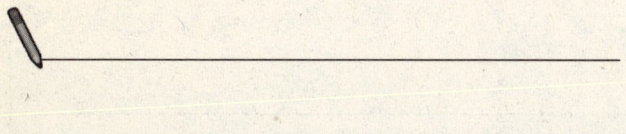

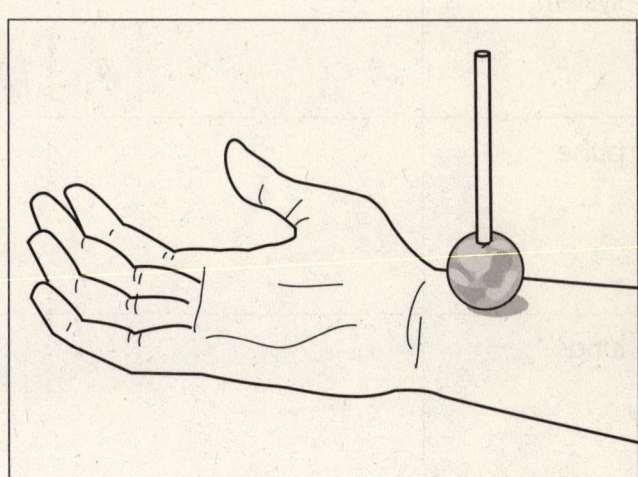

☑ **5.** Measure your pulse for 30 seconds. Record.

Explain Your Results

6. Infer what made the straw move.

_____

_____

7. What can your pulse tell you about your heart?

_____

_____

_____

_____

Building a Spirometer

STEM Connection: Technology

NASA modeled firefighter equipment after the life support systems used by astronauts. The system includes a face mask, frame and harness, a warning device, and an air tank.

Help From Space

A house catches fire. Before plunging into the building, firefighters put on tanks and masks. This equipment allows them to breathe amid the smoke and flames. In that way, firefighters are like astronauts. Both work in places where oxygen is limited. Both need special equipment to help them breathe. Both use equipment designed by NASA.

Firefighter breathing equipment used to be very heavy. It was so heavy that many firefighters did not use it. As a result, many firefighters were hurt from breathing in too much smoke.

NASA decided to help. Its scientists had made lightweight breathing equipment for its astronauts. They adapted that same technology for firefighters.

The NASA-designed gear weighs much less than the old equipment. This makes it easier and more comfortable for firefighters to wear. That means fewer firefighters are injured from breathing in smoke.

Take It Further

Firefighters are not the only people who have benefited from space technology. NASA has created technology used in hospitals, airports, and even in your own home. Visit the NASA Solutions website to see how America's space program benefits you. Explore the many ways NASA technology affects daily life. Then use this information to make a presentation describing the NASA technology in your own life.

Living in Space

Being in space has unusual effects on the human body. Muscles and bones lose strength. Fluids travel differently through the body, giving astronauts puffy faces and skinny legs. Keeping astronauts safe and healthy is a big job.

The scientists and engineers who do this big job work in bioastronautics. Bioastronautics is the study of how to support life in space. It includes life science, medical, and engineering training. Bioastronautics helped determine how much oxygen astronauts need every day. Building the oxygen machine for the space station also used bioastronautics.

There is still much bioastronautics work to do. Scientists and engineers continue to explore ways to improve life in space.

Take It Further

Bioastronautics plays a role in every part of astronaut life. Visit the Japanese Aerospace Exploration Agency (JAXA) website in English. Select "For Students." Click on "Life in Space." Explore each aspect of space life. Write a diary entry from the viewpoint of an astronaut. Describe how you would stay safe and healthy while in space.

Astronauts must exercise every day to prevent muscle loss. Scientists use bioastronautics to determine the type and amount of exercise needed. Engineers use bioastronautics to design space-friendly exercise equipment like this treadmill.

STEM Connection: Engineering Career

Introduction

Breathing in Space

What would it be like to live in space? Imagine floating from room to room. Picture looking out your window and seeing Earth below you. But how would you breathe? There is no oxygen in space and people cannot live without oxygen. The crew of the International Space Station generates their own oxygen. How do they do this? They have a machine that separates oxygen out of water. What happens if the machine breaks? How do the astronauts breathe? In case of emergency, the space station also stores large tanks of oxygen. These tanks can be used while the astronauts repair their oxygen machine.

Take It Further

Go to the NASA International Space Station website, multimedia page, and click on "3D Resources." Navigate to the Station Spacewalk Game. Read the instructions and then play the game. Can you complete your mission before you run out of oxygen?

The International Space Station uses a machine to generate oxygen. On Earth, oxygen is released by plants. What are the benefits of each oxygen source? What are the challenges?

STEM

Engineering

Engineering is using science to solve real-world problems.

Engineers find ways to meet our needs.

They apply scientific knowledge to build and improve technology.

You can use engineering to solve problems too.

Math

Math is a useful tool.

It can help you understand your data better. You can use charts and graphs to organize your data. You can use math to summarize your data.

People use math to solve problems in science, technology, and engineering.

What Is STEM?

At school, you probably have separate math classes, science classes, and English classes. But, can you use English in math class? Of course you can! You can use what you learn in one class to help you understand another. Applying what you learn is a big part of STEM: Science, Technology, Engineering and Math.

Science

Science is a way of learning about the world. Scientists observe nature.

They ask questions and conduct experiments to find out about nature.

They communicate their results to help us understand our world.

Technology

Technology is all around you.

It is not just computers and TVs.

Your pen, your pack, and even your shoes are examples of technology.

Technology is how people change the world to meet their needs.

Build and Test a Prototype

Next, engineers build the solution they chose. This working model is called a prototype. Engineers test their prototype. They take measurements and collect data. Then they use the data to find out what works well. For example, they might try to find out if their solution is safe, sturdy, and easy to use.

Find Problems and Redesign

Engineers also test the model to find out what is not working well. They identify problems. They redesign the model to make it work better. Most designs need some changes before they are final.

Communicate the Solution

Engineers need to tell the people who build and use the product about the final design. They do this in different ways. They can make detailed drawings. They can write descriptions. They can organize their data in tables and graphs. Whatever they do, they must communicate their results in clear and precise ways.

What stage of the design process is this person completing?

The Engineering Design Process

Engineers are people who solve problems. They use the engineering design process described below to make new products. They may not follow these steps in the same order each time.

Identify a Need

When making a new product, engineers start by identifying a need or problem. Maybe a product is not working well. Maybe people need a new product. Engineers choose a problem or need to work on.

Research the Problem

Then, engineers gather information. They may find articles on the internet. They may find information in books and magazines. They may talk to other engineers. They might even conduct tests.

Design a Solution

Engineers use their research to find new solutions. Teams of engineers brainstorm ideas. During brainstorming, team members suggest design solutions. Often, one suggestion leads to other ideas.

As the team works, they take notes carefully. They write down all their ideas, sources, and material lists. They can use this information later if they need to. Or, others can use the notes to help them repeat the process.

Brainstorming usually results in many possible solutions. But engineers cannot build all these possible designs. They need to choose the best solution. To help them, they think about limits to their designs. Money and time are common limits.

Engineers also make trade-offs. In a trade-off, engineers trade one benefit of a design for another. For example, they might want to lower the cost of the product. To do this, they might use weaker materials. After making trade-offs and thinking about limits, engineers will choose the best solution.

Building a Spirometer

Project STEM

Introduction to STEM
The Engineering Design Process . . . . ivS
What Is STEM? . . . . viS

Building a Spirometer
Introduction to Breathing in Space . . . . viiiS
Engineering Career *Living in Space* . . . . ixS
Technology *Help From Space* . . . . xS
Quick Lab *Measuring Your Pulse* 1S
Vocabulary Practice 2S
Math Practice *Mental Math: Multiplying* 3S
STEM Project *Breath of Life* 4S
Career Spotlight *Biomedical Engineer* 9S
Hands-on Inquiry *What Do You Breathe Out?* 11S
Technology Zone *Getting Oxygen in Space* 12S
Enrichment *Your Respiratory System* 14S
Assessment *Breathing in Space* 15S
Performance Assessment *A Spirometer for Everyone* 17S
Standardized Test Prep 18S

Appendices
Scientific Methods

Making Measurements

Safety Tips and Contract*

Review the Safety Tips and Contract before beginning each topic.

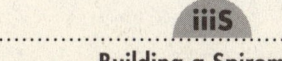

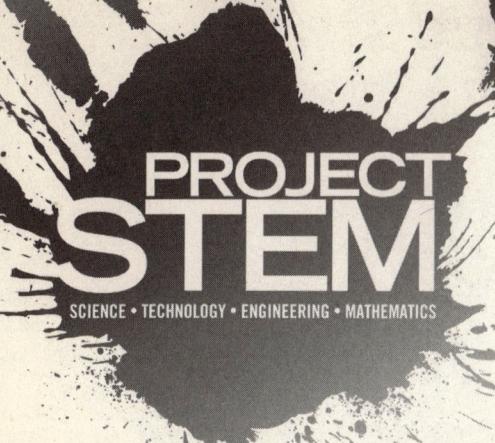

Building A Spirometer

Grades 3–5

Glenview, Illinois • Boston, Massachusetts • Chandler, Arizona • Upper Saddle River, New Jersey

ALWAYS LEARNING   PEARSON